Richard Deacon Out of Order

Contents

Published by Tate St Ives
Supported by the Henry Moore Foundation
and Tate St Ives' Members
Edition 2000

Richard Deacon In Between

In 2001 Richard Deacon developed a large installation of steamed, curved, organic wooden forms which filled the gallery for his exhibition at Dundee Contemporary Arts in Scotland. The remarkable installation, *UW84DC* (2001), built on previous explorations of dynamic wooden forms and continued to explore his various ongoing preoccupations in his sculpture. Some of these are; the relationship between body and space and the spaces in-between, the multiplicity of metaphorical and/or literal readings, and the complexities of inner and exterior space, shadow and shine in his works. *UW84DC* is notable for its grouped complex single forms – some open, some closed – which appear, in one sense, to refer to the serpentine complexities of an ocean's surface rendering the visual weight of spaces between the forms, whilst playing with the restricted nature of our vision in terms of how we see the near and far.

Deacon is curious about how the human eye reacts to the spatial complexities of forms. We cannot ever 'see' an object in its entirety,

so in a sense a fragment of what we see is the 'real' experience, part is remembered (from walking around the form to see it) and part is an interiorising or 'imagining' of the form. In between we have to make a visual and conceptual leap of faith to interpret the spatial complexities of the sculpture. In *UW84DC* we can see his attraction to a curvilinear language of open and broken forms that coalesce and break down, seeming to suggest coherence and chaos simultaneously.

Deacon's installation in three galleries and the courtyard of Tate St Ives establishes an exciting spatial dynamic within its complex architecture which plays with the viewer's interaction with sculpture in its making and placing. The large hand-built ceramic works *Flower* (2004), *Another Kind of Blue* (2005) and the series *Gap #1-8* (2004) – assembled from cut up thrown elements – are finished with a very rich glaze which suggests a relationship both with painting and landscape. These are new forms of an unexpected scale and surface that –

incidentally – both disrupt and embody notions of beauty derived from nature.

Individual (2004) and *Restless* (2005), show Deacon's continuing preoccupation with the concept of emergence as a property of complex systems (in keeping with his fascination for the instability of form – the non-shape represented in cloud formations and flowing water). In contrast with their predecessor, *UW84DC*, these recent sculptures emphasise their fabrication with their broader curves, wide metal 'stays' and multiple sawn and screwed sections. The newest evolution in this series is the torqued or twisted beam controlling an unfurling or previously wrapped set of curves which are seriously 'willed' into position. Looped and bent wood is pinned under pressure and the resulting forms suggest the graceful coherence of a dynamic, (albeit restrained and dangerous), sea.

Deacon has said that 'idleness can be fruitful' speaking of the moments when, in repose, how we have a natural tendency to doodle on paper or play with small, unimportant things that come to hand such as elastic bands or paper clips. It is the seemingly small and unimportant aspects of play which continue to feed the evolution of Deacon's sculpture. All have multiple readings and can never be seen in a single gaze. Their swift evolution means that nothing is ever as it seems at first glance as Deacon continues to seek the elusive and changing forms which challenge our understanding of his work.

I want to thank a number of Tate colleagues for their contribution to the exhibition; Rosie Freemantle, Jack Warans, Kate Parsons, Norman Pollard and the technical team as well as Kerry Rice, Arwen Fitch and Sara Hughes.

We are thankful to the Henry Moore Foundation and Tate St Ives members for their essential financial support, allowing us to have more ambition in the making of this exhibition.

The filmmakers Stewart Wilson and Paul Hookham of KSA have filmed extensively the complex processes underpinning the making of Deacon's sculptures and completed a short but revelatory film commissioned by Tate St Ives. We are also very grateful to Matthew Perry who produces Deacon's wooden sculptures, to Niels Dietrich and Anna Zimmermann, his collaborators in ceramic in Cologne and to Gary Chapman at Twin Engineering for his insights into working with stainless steel.

In his excellent essay Edmund de Waal brings new readings of Deacon's ceramic pieces from his position as an artist who uses clay. Clarrie Wallis' eloquent text contributes to our understanding of the links and complexities of Deacon's thinking and making. We are grateful to both authors for their participation.

Most importantly, we are grateful to Richard Deacon for his collaborative spirit in shaping this presentation of his sculpture and his dedication to creating new works for this distinguished exhibition.

Susan Daniel-McElroy Director

This page
Detail from **Gap #8**
2004
Glazed ceramic
20 x 105 x 71 cm
Courtesy Lisson Gallery, London
© the Artist

Page 7
Another Kind Of Blue
2005
Glazed ceramic
85 x 237 x 60 cm
Courtesy Lisson Gallery, London
© the Artist

Page 9
Detail from **Gap #8**

Page 13
Gap #1-8
Installation,
Tate St Ives, 2005

Do you see yonder cloud that's almost in the shape of a camel?

By the mass, and 'tis like a camel, indeed.

Methinks it is like a weasel.

It is backed like a weasel.

Or like a whale?

Very like a whale.

(Hamlet Act 3 Scene 2)

Very Like a Whale The Sculpture of Richard Deacon

Much of Richard Deacon's sculpture has Hamlet's wayward territory as its subject. Deacon's attention to the moments of transition, to the shape-shifting of clouds, the flux of ideas, the changing intonations of speech or song, continues to make his sculpture particularly difficult to describe. It is the problem of suggestiveness, the strength that we hear implicit in Hamlet's insistent voice: describe that cloud, mark it, map it, capture it. Find a way of holding that cloud, transitory and inchoate as it is. Present it in another way: name it, unname it, rename it.

There does not seem to be a critical language that is appropriately responsive to this tide of images. How can one do justice to the accumulative, meandering, vestigial, ancillary, accretive, dream-like experience of standing in front of Deacon's sculpture, or walking round it? How can you plot the way in which images ebb and flow and ideas precede each other, recede from each other? How can you connect the tension between the planned, coherent, judicial, measured side of Deacon's work with the metaphorical slide into other forms, the suggestiveness to other states and forms that is so present?

Perhaps we should end up with simple lists, make a long, sinuous line of transitive verbs, as the young Richard Serra did in a notebook in 1967:

to roll

to crease

to fold

to store

to bend

to shorten

to twist

to twine

to dapple

to dapple

to crumple

to shave

to tear

to chip

to split

to cut...[1]

Deacon's attitude is subtly but significantly different. His array of transitive verbs is more extensive, (we might add to glue to rivet to fire to melt) but it is in the specificity of his attitudes to material that he is so very particular.

For the last few years Deacon has been working with great intensity with clay. His well-known catholicity with materials (resins, laminated woods, leather, carpet, metals, linoleum, glass), now includes a substantial body of ceramic work. These new sculptures have been shown in exhibitions in Germany and in London. For his exhibition at Tate St Ives he has made a vast and complex installation piece *Gap #1-8* (2004), and two huge singular forms, *Flower* (2004) and *Another Kind of Blue* (2005). Deacon's work with clay is not an easy or homogenous body of work to critique: it plays none of the obvious cards of significance that artists have used when dealing with clay. It is not overtly gestural (as with Anish Kapoor's opening up of solid masses of red clay) nor overtly referential to vessels (as with Nicholas Pope's sculptures for The oratory of heavenly space).[2] In fact it is difficult to think of other artists who have started to use clay and have not been in some way seduced by its complex matrix of messiness and inchoateness, the way in which it shifts its states from liquid to solid, the way in which it moves. Clay is inexhaustible stuff. It is cheap.

It has little value in the hierarchy of materials: it proclaims itself as demotic, basic, primal. It is earth. As earth it is universal but also particular: it comes out of territory, land, place. To work with it is to make something out of nothing. It is an act of Ur-creation: 'God gave man a little bit of mud' in Gauguin's words.[3] It is possible to use clay to record the passage of one moment of one person through the world, to sketch, to mark in an abbreviated way the flux of feeling. Because of this the cultural history of artists using clay is one of them rediscovering immediacy. The images of Lucio Fontana pushing a long pole into a mass of clay to create an interior space, of Picasso bending the just-thrown neck of a pot at Vallauris, or of Asger Jorn riding his scooter over a playground of clay to create large random markings, are the images that tell this story. The connection between the body and the material is transcribed as speed. Speed is then transcribed as authentic experience. We could say that the narrative of twentieth century clay is of artists being experiential – from Gauguin and Nolde to Noguchi and Cragg.

Deacon's ceramic sculpture is of a different order. It is slower. He is interested in how clay moves, but not in the intelligible hand mark, the signifier of authenticity. He is interested in how clay fires, but not in the gestural markings of a wood-kiln, the signifier of robust vernacular identity. Deacon works with the German ceramics studio (Werkstatte fur Bildhauerei) of

Nils Dietrich. Dietrich's studio in Cologne has at its core a small, highly-experienced team of ceramicists that collaborates with an extraordinary group of artists and architects that include Deacon, Thomas Schütte, Rosemarie Trockel, Daniel Liebeskind and Norbert Prangenburg amongst others. There is no British equivalent to Dietrich and, indeed, the only other non-institutional ceramics studio that is remotely comparable is that of Hans Spinner, who works with Chillida, Caro and Tapies.[4] But where Spinner provides an opportunity for artists to make highly gestural work, and fire it in a wood-fired kiln to create distinctive flame marks, Dietrich's studio has no house style. It is highly proficient at creating large ceramic structures, but each artist's work is distinct.

Two huge kilns dominate the upper floor space. Below are innumerable crated pieces, banks of stacked clay bags, a library of thousands of glaze and clay body tests. Here too are the small clay pieces, 'core pieces', that Deacon has made, some in terracotta, others in a white clay body. Some are squeezed pieces of clay – not maquettes but starting points for conversations with himself and with the studio. Others are complex geometric forms carved out of solid pieces of clay, others have the deeply inscribed marks that appear on *Flower* (2004). 'Ribbon pieces', small sculptures that look as if they have kinship with pipes, wait to be lustred gold and silver.

On the winter day on which I accompanied Deacon to the studio, a fug of melting chocolate enveloped us. Various complex sculptures by Deacon, Louise Bourgeois and Mike Kelley (a leg) were being cast in chocolate. Vats of chocolate bubbled away. A new clay piece of Deacon's was being constructed in the middle of the floor. Another sculpture had been bisque-fired and was waiting to be glazed by him. It was apparent that Deacon worked in a highly particular way in this studio: it seemed to be mutually interrogative. Questions were going in all directions. The largest horizontal kiln had just been opened, the firing chamber suspended on pulleys above it. Sitting inside on three huge kiln shelves was Deacon's newest piece *Another Kind of Blue* (2005).

It was vast. In terms of technique it was a brilliant accomplishment: a hermetic, single volume that seemed to shift its weight as you went round it. It comprises a series of planes with the surface given over to a series of blues. Plural colours: it was very definitely a painterly glazed surface, rather than an industrial glazed surface. It seemed to echo Malevich's Suprematist ceramics: Malevich's fierce white planes superceded by Deacon's fierce blues.[5] Where his earlier series from 2001/02, *Kind of Blue*, were open structures made up of repeated formal structures – tubes, ellipses – this offered no apparent way in. You wanted to go round and round it to see how the different planes met up. It felt both satisfyingly complete, a thing in itself, and yet quizzical. A little

1 Richard Serra quoted in Rosalind E Krauss Passages in *Modern Sculpture*, MIT 1981 page 276.

2 cf *Slip: Artists in the Netherlands and Britain working with ceramic*, De Hallen/Sainsbury Centre for Visual Arts 2002.

3 *Gauguin by Himself*, edited by Belinda Thomson, London 2004 page 74 cf also Merete Bodelsen *Gauguin's Ceramics*, London 1964.

4 cf Garth Clark *Hans Spinner*, New York 2002.

like Hamlet's whale. This was all the more compelling because with Deacon's sculpture we feel we should know, and understand, the ordering of the making, the building of his sculpture. Even if it is a chimera we have come to expect that way in: the rivets, the glue at the joints, the stitching. Its all there for us to see: the fabrication is transparent. With this piece its hiddeness was startling and affecting. And with ceramic it is doubly so as ceramic has made such a virtue out of its transparency.

Also at the studio was the 2004/05 piece *The One Behind the Kiln*, or *Throw*. It is an open honeycomb structure made up of repeated thrown cylinders stacked on their sides so as to produce myriad view points. Some views are clear, some are blocked. Some of the edges are broken, giving the sense that it could be part of a greater whole. It is clearly made of hand-made components, but the repetition is on the cusp between the industrial and the organic. It is a map of voids, a chart of interiors, a structure constructed from absences. Deacon has a long interest in how to contain space: his work with welded polycarbonate, or his bentwood sculptures have often played with ideas of how to contain volumes. This is the repeated drama that we are invited to witness. But like many of Deacon's most compelling works, it is the pull between the detailed passages of lyricism (the pooling and fluxing of glazes, the interstices between the joined elements) and the cerebral nature of the overall

structure that is so exciting. This is the sensation that the American philosopher John Dewey in his seminal book *Art and Experience* anatomised as the flight and perchings of a bird – the pull between the activity of the eye and its rest. Dewey stressed the repetitiveness of this activity, suggesting that in a great work of art this experience was endless.[6] In this piece of Deacon's there are a series of unfolding images and ideas. Firstly it is iterative: it reflects the nature of repetition itself. Secondly it is about making, but it is also about dismantling: it is a piece whose fragmentary nature might indicate that it is still being made or still being unmade. Thirdly its imagery is unsettling. It oscillates between stacked scrolls, and the stacked bones of an ossuary. Even Deacon's titles for it oscillate between the highly particular and the expansively general.

This unsettled feeling was present in the endless conversation about the placing of the work, watching the placing of the work. The one behind the kiln…the one in the kiln…This was more than curatorial dexterity, acuity about where the work looked best, worked hardest, it was more the knowledge that how you approached the sculpture changed your responses radically to it. This is something that Deacon has always concerned himself with, playing with expectations and framing devices for his sculpture. Recently in his curation with Clarrie Wallis and Lizzie Carey Thomas of the exhibition of medieval sculpture *Image And Idol* at Tate Britain in 2001/02

he challenged both the conventions of display (plinths work only in this way) and the idea that you can re-display. Given how engaged he is with movement it is no surprise Deacon encourages movement around his sculpture, but also through it,

as with his sculpture *Red Sea Crossing* in the Marian Goodman Gallery in New York in 2004. This is intriguing because we are used to white cube spaces being admonitory, asensual, asomatic temples, an apparatus for 'single-sense epiphanies' as an American critic put it.[7] Deacon wants epiphanies to be fully embodied.

This unease is even clearer in *Gap #1-8* (2004). This is a series of undulating forms made from thrown and joined components that are to be placed near each other to make up an installation that will stretch through the great curved vitrine in Tate St Ives. They are forms that are on the move, slightly ameoboid 'a visual meditation on the logic of organic growth itself' to borrow the words of Rosalind Krauss.[8] Open at both top and base, you are highly aware of the forms as a kind of three dimensional drawing in space. Their volume, their vesselness, is displaced. Near to each other they give the impression of pushing and pulling, of systole and diastole. The cuts or vents that mark the points of transition let the air in and let the air out. This work could have been made from extruded sections of clay, cut up and pasted together. But it is made from thrown vessels – superbly thrown by his German

5 cf Nina Lobanov-Rostovsky *Revolutionary Ceramics Soviet Porcelain 1917-1927*, London 1990.
6 John Dewey *Art as Experience*, New York 1934 page 17.
7 Barbara Kirschenblatt-Gimlett quoted in *Empire of the Senses*, edited by David Howes Berg 2005 page 267.

8 Krauss ibid page 253.
9 Richard Deacon *In Praise of Television: Television and Representation*, Association des Amis du Musee Departemental de Rochechouart, 1998. Revised 2000.

10 James Elkins *Our Beautiful, Dry, and Distant Texts*, London 2000 pp 175-178.
11 Deacon quoted in *Undetermined Pleasure and Unnecessary Beauty* An interview with Ian Tromp *Sculpture Magazine* Nov 1999 vol 18 no 9.
12 Elkins ibid page 176.

ceramic assistant Anna Zimmerman – where the curve is always the same, but the top and bottom radius are different.

In *Gap #1-8* you have a strong sense of play. One of the aspects of play is an upending of the linearity of narrative: endings are not discrete, they are generative and provisional. It is this sense of the provisional rather than the emphatic, the contingent rather than the rooted that mark out Deacon's sculpture. As he wrote in 1996 of a sequence of images, it 'is constructed by association, one thing leading to another in a variety of ways. The images, of complex shapes or momentary or indefinite events, allow this kind of associative interconnectivity. Complex and allusive patterns have often been used as signifiers or portents, whether of the weather or of gods: or of the actions of armies, or of individuals. Clouds, smoke, entrails, the flight of birds, the fall of sticks, the spread of tea leaves, the scatter of dust: such patterns are divined, the future is guessed. Randomness (or complexity) allows for reading, opens horizons of possibilities..' [9] In a parallel way Miro, Picasso and Fontana all upended the rootedness of ceramic objects and treated vessels as in some ways found objects, susceptible to the conditions of surrealist exchange, randomness. Vessels were starting points, not conclusions. Deacon takes this on, and uses the memory of the thrown pottery vessel within the work. *Gap #1-8* is 'associative interconnectivity': it is also a subtle and rather beautiful use of a material that has been through a process.

Thrown clay – like laminated wood – is a stressed material that has a memory. It moves. It meanders.

'Meandering' is what the art historian James Elkins in his book on the writing of art history, *Our Beautiful, Dry and Distant Texts*, discusses in his attempt to recover creative possibilities in writing. Elkins, perturbed by the faux rigour of contemporary art history with its dogmatic sets of rhetoric, sets out to enjoy the experiences, the 'rhythms... general directions...swerves and turns' that he encounters in writing on art. He is particularly attentive to Deacon's 'one thing leading to another', quoting Webster's definition approvingly that to meander is to 'wander aimlessly or casually and without urgent destination', in this case 'among the works and texts of the history of art.' He suggests that shifting, unpredictable encounters are creative. Furthermore he suggests that 'Meandering is…geometrically complex. A person who is meandering does not accomplish directed work, such as mapping, building or surveying; each of those activities is more programmatic than meandering.' It is also 'furtively autobiographical': 'the patterns of moving, pausing, sitting, glancing, and moving on all find voice in the narrative and…in the succession of narratives on a single object the kinds of tradition I have been sampling.' And fourthly 'like art history, meandering is inconsistent even though it can appear deliberate. A meandering stream is an inconstant thing, sometimes flooding its banks, other times receding and forming

short-lived islands, or creating brakes and backwaters, and always dividing and redividing itself'. [10]

This is a great correspondence with Deacon's approach to the metaphoric possibilities of meandering. Deacon has written that 'the classic example is the turbulent flow in certain liquids – there's a point where the liquid is moving too fast for there to be anything coherent about it and another point where the liquid is moving slowly and it's entirely coherent. But there's a point between these two at which ordered pattern emerges, in the form of vortices, ripples, and eddies. This is what interests me, this openness that emerges between those two states – it's not to do with generating a pattern from a mathematical program, it's to do with this point of transition between order and disorder, where different kinds of ordering emerge.' [11] Elkins' uncovering of a narrative of meandering within the writing of art history, with its powerful imaging of flowing water has a direct parallel with Deacon's apprehension that his sculpture, geometrically complex, unprogrammatic, full of swerves and turns, is concerned with a 'different kind of ordering.'

Deacon's new sculpture in clay is compelling. Those moments when movement – spatial or linguistic – are captured, are moments of great beauty. They are contingent moments, ceasuras rather than full stops, 'fictions of stability' [12] places where it is possible – indeed necessary – to see constancy even when we are well aware of flux.

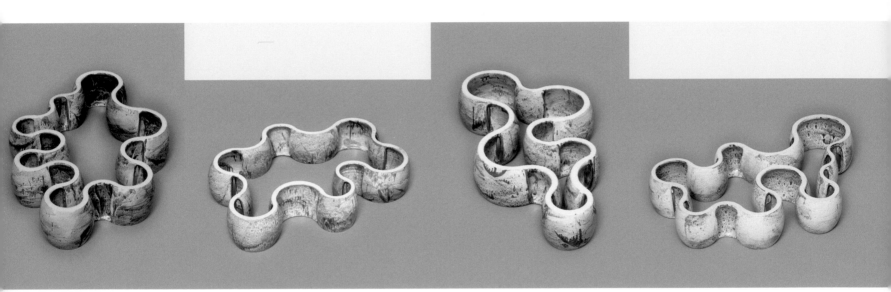

Gap #8   Gap #7   Gap #6   Gap #5

Gap #1-8
2004
Glazed ceramic
Dimensions variable
Courtesy Lisson Gallery, London
© the Artist

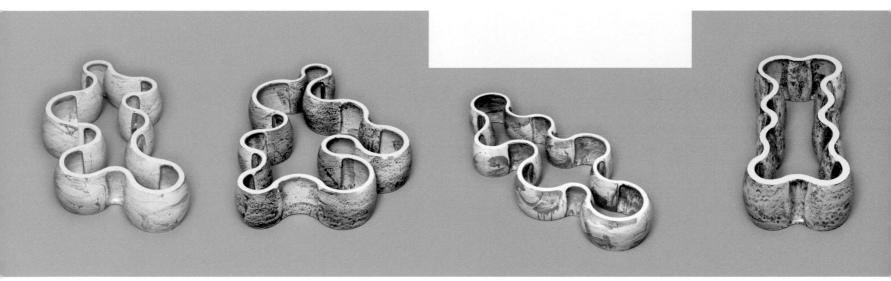

Gap #4   Gap #3   Gap #2   Gap #1

Gap #8
2004
Glazed ceramic
20 x 105 x 71 cm
Courtesy Lisson Gallery, London
© the Artist

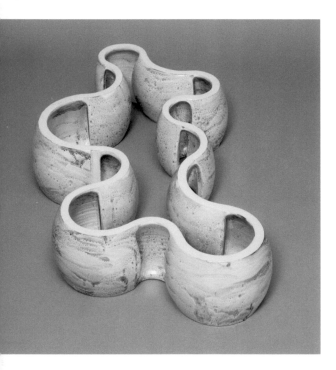

Left
Gap #4
2004
Glazed ceramic
20 x 108 x 65 cm
Courtesy Lisson Gallery, London
© the Artist

Opposite page
Detail from **Gap #4**

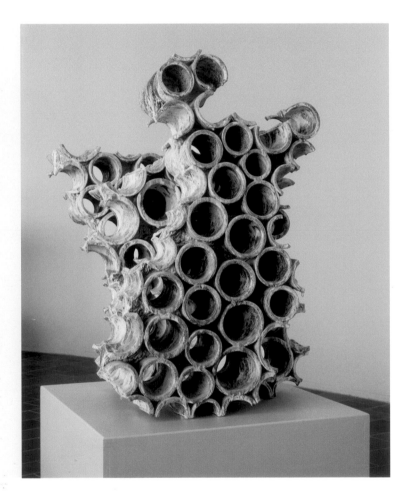

Left
Throw
2004
Ceramic
106 x 60 x 85 cm
Courtesy Lisson Gallery, London
© the Artist

Opposite page
Flower 2
2004
Glazed ceramic
84 x 121 x 89 cm
Courtesy Lisson Gallery, London
© the Artist

1
2

1

1
Another Kind Of Blue
2005
Glazed ceramic
85 x 237 x 60 cm
Courtesy Lisson Gallery, London
© the Artist

2
Flower 2
2004
Glazed ceramic
84 x 121 x 89 cm
Courtesy Lisson Gallery, London
© the Artist

3
Masters of the Universe #1
2005
Stainless steel
163 x 194 x 126 cm
Courtesy Lisson Gallery, London
© the Artist

Out of Order

In August 2000 Richard Deacon exhibited *Umhh* a new sculpture at the project space *Fig-1*.[1] Reminiscent of apple peel that has been casually dropped on the floor, this sculpture represented a significant development in Deacon's distinctive sculptural language and acts as an important precedent for the wooden works included in this exhibition. Each ribbon-like component is made from a compilation of strips of ash that have been meticulously steam-bent into a repertoire of shapes and then screwed together to form evocative loops and curls. In this way structure and form are direct consequences of the process of making and assembly and the basic properties of the material. If shape and surface appear as one, the visibility of the screw heads offers an interesting difference between, or means of transgression of, the inside and the outside of the sculpture. While charting the terrain between space and structure they also emphasise the discrepancy between interior and exterior of the swirls of wood and allow

possibilities for revision of inside to outside. If *Umhh* (2000) established new parameters in terms of working with materials, this vocabulary was further developed by *UW84DC* (2001) (You Wait for the Sea) a group of fifteen works that were shown together the following year at Dundee Contemporary Art. Here these combinations or sequences were built into unique forms that anticipate the organisational principles of recent wooden sculptures such as *Out of Order* (2003) and *Slippery When Wet* (2004). Individual elements are again connected together by small tabs that act as an important counterpoint to the twisting and turning forms and introduce an additional sense of rhythm, or musical notation. The work emerges from the repetition of these methods. This process in some respects echoes the artist's procedure for the making of an important series of early drawings *It's Orpheus When There's Singing* (1978-9). In both instances, elements emerge from a rigorous, formal and quite abstract

procedure, where the curve and the counter curve are particularly important. As the artist described in his notebooks of the time, each drawing began with a geometric figure: 'a spiral links points on the figure. A series of arcs and curves partially tied to the spiral is sprung off various points inside and outside the figure. The development of these curves builds up a network or ground against which specific shapes are allowed to emerge.'[2] Thus the process of making allows the work to be autonomous.

Relationships between body and space, between interior and exterior, self and other have preoccupied Deacon throughout his career. Since the late 1970s he has made objects that further explore relations between the literal and the metaphoric. In early sculptures like *For Those Who Have Ears #2* (1983), form is often described not by its shape but by its boundary or edge. It is the interface between interior and exterior that is important, the divide between surface

Below
It's Orpheus When There's Singing #7
1978-9
Pastel and pencil on paper
111.7 x 147 cm
Tate
© the Artist

Right
Umhh
2000
Steamed ash
Dimensions variable
© the Artist
Photo: S White

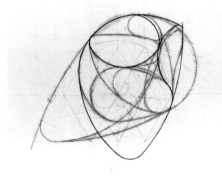

For Those Who Have Ears #2
1983
Laminated wood and adhesive
273 x 400 x 110 cm
Tate
© the Artist

UW84DC #1 - 15
2001
Steamed ash and aluminium
Dimensions variable
Installation View, DCA
(Dundee Contemporary Arts)
© the Artist
Photo: Colin Ruscoe

Left
Detail from **Slippery When Wet**
2004
Steamed ash and stainless steel
223 x 382 x 198 cm
The Würth Museum, Germany
© the Artist
Photo: Joaquín Cortés

Below left
Nicolas Poussin
Landscape with a Man killed by a Snake
probably 1648
Oil on canvas
119.4 x 198.8 cm
© The National Gallery

Below
Leonardo da Vinci
**Studies of water passing obstacles
and falling into a pool**
c. 1508-9
Windsor Leoni volume 12660V
The Royal Collection
© 2005, Her Majesty Queen Elizabeth II

Opposite page
Slippery When Wet

and edge, form and image, the real and the imagined. If the contours of *UW84DC* also describe a series of open shapes in space, they articulate Deacon's fascination with the dialectic of inside and outside in a new way. Unlike most of Deacon's earlier work twelve of the fifteen sculptures have open ends – the sequence of curls and spirals does not complete an enclosure.

Made in groups of four or five, Deacon always intended that the sculptures would be seen together in the first instance and that the spaces between each component to be as important as the work themselves. To this end, he rented a separate studio to make this work and was thus able to keep an eye on the whole thing as it developed, creating a work that somehow balances volume and space. With *UW84DC*, the complex, serpentine forms play with the viewer's sense and experience of nearness and distance. The result is a sea of twisting and turning elements which covers the expanse of the gallery floor, heaving like a seething body of water, seeming to move in all directions at once. It has the effect of both confronting the viewer yet also withdrawing into the distance, of being 'too close together to be seen as separate yet too far apart to be one thing'.[3]

The installation also explores compositional issues relating to the notion of depth, surface and structure, figure and ground. This interest can in part be traced back to Deacon's writings on a painting by Poussin, *Landscape with a Man killed by a Snake* (1648), in which he addresses the relationship between representation and the experience of spatial illusion.[4] His curiosity with looking at how imagery can help explain spatial issues, for example the expression of deep and shallow space within two dimensions has also been probed by his collages of photographs and ink on paper drawings. However *UW84DC's* twisting and sweeping curves and the dynamic yet carefully controlled structuring of the installation, conjures up a sense of Baroque movement and figuration present in *Landscape with a Man killed by a Snake*. In this work Poussin achieves a unique and engaging spatial effect where the terror of the sight of the serpent draping the horizontal body provokes a visual energy or disturbance that 'ripples through the rest of the painting'.[5] Drawn into *UW84DC's* midst, its writhing forms have something of an equivalent sense of vitality or animation, which encompasses the viewer. Elsewhere, Deacon has suggested that 'being alive and being dead are connected to curved, counter curved and straight'[6] the energy that abounds in nature. If the open-ended curve creates a sense of motion – of life, the rigid line, in this instance of Poussin's corpse, is its antithesis.

Deacon's attraction to a curvilinear, organic visual language also extends into an interest in the spiral or helix – from the structure of

plants and shells to molecular structures of biological systems. He has described how an aerial photograph he took of a spiral formation in the River Tay, Dundee, acted as an important catalyst for this latest body of work. At the time when Deacon was originally developing his lexis of shapes he also made some samples of a square section that were twisted. This experiment in constructing a torsion bend was the result of a feeling of dissatisfaction with form-making that is the product of bending and folding in one plane and a wish to find a new way of moving around in space. The resultant barley sugar twist has proven to be an important and technically challenging element of this new vocabulary. For example, in the complex dynamics of *Out of Order* (2003), all parts begin and end at the twists. Built piece-meal, Deacon was interested in 'using the twisted core as a start and finish point for the other assemblies of curves'.[7] Sometime after that he 'realised that the separate elements could be linked together, that there was a way in which the twisted pieces could be joined end to end to form a single line like a loose loop of string, supported by and supporting the loops and curves that spring off them'.[8]

Deacon is particularly interested in the concept of emergence as a property of complex systems. This is in keeping with his fascination with the 'non-shape', the unstable boundary or threshold between formed and unformed, which has been a consistent line of enquiry in recent years.[9]

He has described how he looked a great deal at images connected with transitional states such as cloud formations as well as the ways in which uncertainty has been represented – for example, the *Deluge Drawings* (c1515-17) by Leonardo da Vinci that depict the effects of whirlwinds, floods, hurricanes and storms. *Studies of Passing Obstacles and Falling into a Pool*, (c 1508-9) is a related drawing that predates the Deluge series. It is the result of many closely observed experiments Leonardo undertook to record fluids in motion. The central sketch shows water falling into a pool while in two carefully drawn studies water ebbs and flows around obstructions inserted at various angles into a swiftly moving stream. Deacon's two-part sculpture *Red Sea Crossing* (2003) has somewhat similar characteristics. Made of oak as opposed to ash, a harder wood to manipulate, there is a greater sense of physical tension in the material. Held in place by lengths of twisted 4 x 4 inch beams, complex, ribbon like components or waves, loop and double back on themselves. The sense of force, of materials 'being willed into shape', is compounded by its title, reinforcing the impression of a restrained sea.

In this way we can also understand Deacon's sculptures as an exploration into the concept of plasticity. He has consistently referred to himself as a 'fabricator', where the emphasis is on construction and manipulation and the relationship between the physical and the material. Irrespective

of the medium – wood or clay – the challenge he sets himself grows from the nature of his materials and their relationship to an evolving form. Since 1999 Deacon has been using the workshop of Niels Dietrich in Cologne to make large-scale hand-built ceramic works. The contrast between these unitary forms and the very open structure of the wooden sculptures is particularly important. In both the choice of materials and method of assembling them, Deacon is intent on denying the interiority of the sculpted form – or at least to renounce the interior of forms as a source of their significance.

This rejection of the idea of an 'inside' from which meaning and structure originates is further highlighted by the two wooden works, *Individual* (2004) and *Couple* (2004). As the artist explains both 'are organised around a complex, twisted piece of wood which, rather than forming a perimeter, is a core which generates a zone of influence (in one case) and separation (in the other)… What seems to me to be particularly interesting in the rolling, twisting, bending operations with material [is] that the enclosure or volume created [has] nothing to do with weight or mass, it is empty and therefore connected to meaning in a way that is independent of causality or rationality (that is to say that the outside is not caused by the inside)'.[10] *Individual* is made up of three separate wraps around the twisted core. Self contained, its appearance is suggestive of an organic, molecular structure, in particular the super coiling of

1 *Umhh* was originally presented with a soundtrack prepared by Martin Kreyssig using all the outtakes – all the umhhs – from a long interview made in 1991.
2 Richard Deacon in *Richard Deacon*, Kunstverein Hannover, 1993, page 129.

3 Richard Deacon in conversation with the author, 4 January 2005.
4 Deacon first wrote about this painting in 1977, see Richard Deacon in *Richard Deacon*, Kunstverein Hannover, 1993, page 120. In 1997, twenty years

later he returns to it in relation to *After Poussin*, a work he realised for the Münster Sculpture Project.
5 Richard Deacon in *Skulptur: Projekte in Münster*, 1997; Ed. Klaus Bussmann, Kasper Konig, Florian Matzner; Verlag Gerd Hatje, page 116.

DNA, or an immersion heater. With *Couple* the idea of a twisted section or spine as the initiator of possibilities is developed in a way that the two poles are linked by loops, vaguely similar to electrical charges passing across separate wires. Here Deacon is interested in the space or distance flanked by the two lines, which gives the impression of a system of two equal forces that are parallel and in opposite directions. Neither figurative nor abstract, its title reinforces visual and verbal connections that hint at the link between individuals, between self and other – an association, bond or perhaps sexual encounter.

The swerving, radical bends of *Slippery When Wet* – its title a nod to the road sign – further draw attention to Deacon's preoccupation with the non-linear, or to be more precise, the moment of transition between the two states, linear and non-linear. Enclosed loops, reminiscent of water droplets, spring off from the central twisted backbone – almost as if a cloth has been wrung. Reaching out into the surrounding space, *Slippery When Wet's* baroque twists and convolutions double back on themselves so that the forms oscillate between a state of distressed and the fluid. This potential for a sudden change in behaviour, or passage of one form to another is at the heart of Deacon's interest in the interface or threshold through which ordered complexity emerges – where water turns to ice, or molecules self-organise into a living cell. As he explains: 'The classic example is the turbulent flow in certain liquids: there's a point where the liquid is moving too slowly for there to be anything coherent about it and another point where the liquid is moving fast and it's entirely coherent. But there is also a point between these two at which ordered pattern emerges, in the form of vortices, ripples and eddies. This is what interests me, this openness that emerges between those states – it's not to do with generating a pattern from a mathematical programme, it's to do with a point of transition between order and disorder, where different kinds of ordering emerge.'[11]

In his book *The Fold: Leibniz and the Baroque*,[12] Giles Deleuze reworks the contrast between the Classical and the Baroque. The Classical is a closed regime of perception, with a central focus and produces an effect of clarity, structured around a narrative. By contrast, the Baroque is dynamic and polycentric. Rather than providing a static perspective, the 'centre' continually shifts thus resulting in complex spatial conditions. Mario Perniola's account of the Baroque builds on Deleuze. Perniola first sets up a contrast between the secret and the fold. The secret is a simple truth 'the route to which may be long, complicated and tortuous; but once it is sighted, the secret is effaced'.[13] Though Perniola does not make it explicit this could be seen as the mode of truth of the Classical. By contrast the fold is truth conceived not as an unmasking of a secret but of a complex 'unfolding'; 'the drawing out, the unwinding, the expression of something that is tangled, wound up, gathered in.'[14] It is here that Perniola makes clear the link between the Baroque and the fold. The baroque presents a world of plenitude, of 'folds, complexities and the sinuousness of such a concrete reality'.[15] We have already described the way in which the artist works with his materials, which we can now see as a baroque working with and tracing of the sinuousness of such a concrete reality.

Thus Deacon's work can be seen to demonstrate both a Baroque style and the mode of truth, the fold that the Baroque exemplifies. The works are both literally made up of folds, entanglements and metaphorically the folds of Baroque truth. Moreover, the exploration of the literal and metaphoric, of inside and outside, of figure and ground is not the disclosure of their 'secret' as either form and content but the emergence of complex truths that problematises the very notions of form and content. In this way, his interest in complexity theory is understandable as a shared Baroque sensibility. Stuart Kaufmann, a leading scientist working on the laws of complexity, has characterised the nature of complex systems as entities that are 'tangled and interwoven, dancing together in rhythms, cadences, and profusion'.[16] We might find here a suggestion of the characteristic sensibility of Deacon's work too.

6   e-mail exchange with the author, 11 February 2005.
7   Ibid.
8   Ibid.
9   Penelope Curtis in *Richard Deacon*, Phaidon 2000, page 178.
10 Richard Deacon *À l'Atelier Brancusi: Passage de la Mer Rouge*, Centre Pompidou 2003.
11 Interview with Ian Tromp in *Richard Deacon*, Phaidon Press, 2000, page 158.
12 Giles Deleuze, *The Fold: Leibniz and the Baroque*, Minneapolis: University of Minneapolis Press, 1989.
13 Mario Perniola, *Enigmas*, Verso, 1995, page 4.
14 Ibid, page 5.
15 Ibid, page 6.
16 Stuart Kaufmann, *At Home in the Universe*, Penguin, 1995, page 207.

Red Sea Crossing
2003
Oak and stainless steel
Sculpture in two parts
A: 163 x 345 x 320 cm
B: 204 x 520 x 390 cm
Courtesy Marian Goodman
Gallery, New York
© the Artist
Photo: John Berens, New York

Couple
2004
Steamed ash and stainless steel
221 x 297 x 133 cm
Courtesy Marian Goodman
Gallery, New York
© the Artist
Photo: John Berens, New York

Above
Details from **Individual**
2004
Steamed ash and stainless steel
110 x 314 x 115 cm
Courtesy Marian Goodman
Gallery, New York
© the Artist

Opposite page
Individual

Left
Individual
2004
Steamed ash and stainless steel
110 x 314 x 115 cm
Courtesy Marian Goodman
Gallery, New York
© the Artist

Opposite page
Detail from **Individual**

Foreground
Individual
2004
Steamed ash and stainless steel
110 x 314 x 115 cm
Courtesy Marian Goodman
Gallery, New York
© the Artist

Background
Restless
2005
Steamed ash and stainless steel
158 x 374 x 257 cm
Courtesy Lisson Gallery, London
© the Artist

Page 40-41
Detail from **Restless**

Restless
2005
Steamed ash and stainless steel
158 x 374 x 257 cm
Courtesy Lisson Gallery, London
© the Artist

Restless
2005
Steamed ash and stainless steel
158 x 374 x 257 cm
Courtesy Lisson Gallery, London
© the Artist

Foreground
Restless
2005
Steamed ash and stainless steel
158 x 374 x 257 cm
Courtesy Lisson Gallery, London
© the Artist

Background
Throw
2004
Ceramic
106 x 60 x 85 cm
Courtesy Lisson Gallery, London
© the Artist

Above
Details from **Restless**
(work in progress) 2005
Steamed ash and stainless steel
158 x 374 x 257 cm
Photographed at Matthew Perry Studio
Courtesy Lisson Gallery, London
© the Artist

Opposite page
Restless
(work in progress) 2005

Left
Masters of the Universe #1
2005
Stainless steel
163 x 194 x 126 cm
Courtesy Lisson Gallery, London
© the Artist

Opposite page
Infinity #28
2005
Stainless steel
190 x 160 x 5 cm
Courtesy Lisson Gallery, London
© the Artist

Richard Deacon Selected Biography

Born
Bangor, North Wales

Studied
Somerset College of Art, Taunton, from 1968-69;
St Martins School of Art, London, from 1969-72;
Royal College of Art, London, from 1974-77.
He studied part time at Chelsea School of Art,
London, in 1978.

Lecturing
From 1977-92 Deacon was a visiting lecturer
in sculpture at various art schools, principally
Central School of Art and Design, London;
Chelsea School of Art, London;
Sheffield City Polytechnic;
Bath Academy of Art;
and Winchester School of Art.

Visiting lecturer at Ateliers 63, Haarlem
and Amsterdam (1989-93);
Guest Professor, Hochschule fur Angewande
Kunst, Vienna (1995-96);
and Guest lecturer, MA Programme, Bezalel
Academy of Art and Design, Jerusalem, in 1998.

Deacon has been Visiting Professor at
Chelsea School of Art and the
London Institute since 1992;
Advisor to Rijksakademie van Beelden
Kunsten, Amsterdam, since 1996;
and Professor at Ecole Nationale Superieure
des Beaux Arts, Paris, since 1999.

Exhibitions
Deacon's first one-man show was held in 1978
at The Gallery, Brixton, London. This led to a
string of solo exhibitions, both nationally and
internationally, notably at the Riverside Studios
in 1984, Tate Gallery, London, in 1985,
the Whitechapel Art Gallery, London, in 1988
and at Tate Gallery Liverpool in 1999. He has
exhibited at the Lisson Gallery, London, since
1983, and at Marian Goodman Gallery,
New York, since 1986. Deacon has participated
in many key group exhibitions throughout the
world since 1981.

Awards
Richard Deacon won the Turner Prize,
Tate Gallery, in 1987 and the Robert Jakobsen
Prize, Museum Wurth, Kunzelsau, Germany in
1995. In 1997 he was awarded Chevalier des Arts
et des Lettres, France, and in 1998 was elected
a Royal Academician. Deacon was made CBE
in 1999. In 2005 the University of Leicester
awarded him an honorary doctorate.
He lives and works in London.

Recent solo exhibitions

2004
Slippery When Wet
Galería Distrito Cu4tro, Madrid.

Richard Deacon
Marian Goodman Gallery, New York.

Lead Astray
Recent shared sculptures
New Art Centre and Sculpture Park, Roche Court,
Salisbury, England; Palacio Nacional de Queluz,
Lisbon, Portugal; Yorkshire Sculpture Park,
England (cat.)

Beyond the Clouds
LA Louver, Los Angeles, California.

2003
Made In Cologne – Ceramic sculptures
Museum Ludwig, Cologne, Germany.

Passage de la Mer Rouge
Atelier Brancusi, Centre Pompidou, Paris, France.
Galerie Stadpark, Krems, Austria.

UW84DC
Galerie Thomas Schulte, Berlin.

From Tomorrow
Galeri Susanne Ottesen, Copenhagen.

New Bases
de/di/bY Galerie, Paris

2002
Lisson Gallery, London
Galerie Arlogos, Paris

2001
UW84DC
DCA, Dundee, Scotland
PS1 New York

Between The Two Of Us (with Henk Visch)
Stedelijk Museum, Schiedam, Netherlands

2000
Fig.1, London
L A Louver, Los Angeles

1999
Tate Gallery, Liverpool

1998
Galerie Arlogos, Paris

1997
Marian Goodman Gallery, New York
Musee Departmentale de Rochechouart,
Rochechouart

1996
MACCSI, Caracas (toured to Centro Wilfredo Lam,
Havana; Museo Nacional de Bellas Artes, Buenos
Aires; Museo de Bellas Artes, Santiago de Chile;
Museo Rufino Tamayo, Mexico City)

1995
L A Louver, Los Angeles
Lisson Gallery, London

1994
Customs House, South Shields

1993
Galerie Arlogos, Nantes
Kunstverein Hannover and Orangerie,
Herrenhauser Garten, Hannover

1992
Lisson Gallery, London
Musee d'Art Moderne, Villeneuve d'Ascq.
Marian Goodman Gallery, New York
Museum der Stadt, Waiblingen

1991
Museum Haus Lange and Museum Haus Esters,
Krefeld

1990
Kunstnernes Hus, Oslo
Marian Goodman Gallery, New York
Mala Galerija, Moderna Galerija, Ljublijana

Commissioned projects

2003
Not Out Of The Woods Yet
Building 4, 1st and Howard, San Francisco,
California. Commissioned by Wilson Equity.

2002
Can't See The Wood For The Trees
A9/N22 Neupunkt, Haarlem, Netherlands.
Commissioned by Provincie Noort-Holland.

2000
Just Us
Ocean Plaza, Fuxingmennei St, Beijing, China.

1999
No Stone Unturned
Bemalter Stahl Platz, Liestal, Switzerland.

1996
One Is Asleep, One Is Awake
Tokyo International Forum Building, Tokyo, Japan.

1993
Zeitweise
Mexicoplatz, Vienna, Austria

1992
Between Fiction and Fact
Musee d'Art Moderne, Villeneuve d'Ascq, France

Building From The Inside
Voltaplatz, Krefeld, Germany

This Is Not A Story
Rathausplatz, Waiblingen, Germany

1991
Nobody Here But Us
Office Tower Plaza, Auckland, New Zealand

Let's Not Be Stupid
Former Air Hall Site, University of Warwick,
Coventry, England

1990
Between The Eyes
Yonge Square International Plaza, Toronto, Canada

Once Upon A Time…
Former Redheugh Bridge Abutment,
Gateshead, England

Moor
Victoria Park, Plymouth, England

Publications

1984
Richard Deacon Sculpture 1980-84.
Published by Fruitmarket Gallery and
Le Nouveau Musee. Text, Michael Newman.

1987
Richard Deacon Recent Sculpture 1985-87.
Published by Bonnefanten Museum, Kunstmuseum
Luzern and MUHKA Antwerp. Text Charles Harrison.

1992
Richard Deacon
Carnets de la commande publique, CNAP, Editions
du Regard. Textes de Richard Deacon et Lynne Cooke.

1993
Richard Deacon Sculptures 1987-93
Work Biography 1968-93. Published by Kunstverein
Hannover. Text by Eckhard Schneider. Work
biography compiled by Richard Deacon, Eckhard
Schneider and Dr. Maria Schneider.

1995
Richard Deacon
Monograph published by Phaidon Press
(expanded 2nd edition 2000). Texts by Pier-Luigi
Tazzi, Jon Thompson, Peter Schejeldahl, Mary
Douglas, Richard Deacon and Penelope Curtis.

1999
New World Order/Richard Deacon
Published by Tate Gallery, Liverpool. Texts by
Richard Deacon, Sabine Dylla, Marjorie Allthorpe-
Guyton, Vikki Bell, Phyllis Tuchman, Rui Sanches,
Elisabeth McCrae, Lewis Biggs and Liam Gillick.

2001
Richard Deacon Sculpture
Published by Dundee Contemporary Arts,
Dundee, Scotland. Catalogue texts by Vikki Bell,
Katrina Brown and Andrew Nairne.

2003
Like you know
Richard Deacon Ceramic Sculptures, Gerhard Kolberg
published as catalogue text by Walther Konig for
Museum Ludwig Cologne in Richard Deacon AC.

2005
Slippery When Wet
Published as catalogue to the exhibition at Galería
Distrito Cu4tro, Madrid, Spain. Catalogue essays by
Javier Gonzalez de Durana, Phyllis Tuchmann and
Richard Deacon interview with Kevin Power. Madrid 20.

List of works in exhibition

Ceramic

Another Kind Of Blue 2005
Glazed ceramic
85 x 237 x 60 cm
Courtesy Lisson Gallery, London
© the Artist

Flower 2 2004
Glazed ceramic
84 x 121 x 89cm
Courtesy Lisson Gallery, London
© the Artist

Gap #1-8 2004
Glazed ceramic
Dimensions variable
Courtesy Lisson Gallery, London
© the Artist

Throw 2004
Ceramic
106 x 60 x 85cm
Courtesy Lisson Gallery, London
© the Artist

Stainless steel

Infinity #28 2005
Stainless steel
190 x 160 x 5 cm
Courtesy Lisson Gallery, London
© the Artist

Masters of the Universe #1 2005
Stainless steel
163 x 194 x 126 cm
Courtesy Lisson Gallery, London
© the Artist

Wood

Individual 2004
Steamed ash and stainless steel
110 x 314 x 115 cm
Courtesy Marian Goodman Gallery, New York
© the Artist

Restless 2005
Steamed ash and stainless steel
158 x 374 x 257 cm
Courtesy Lisson Gallery, London
© the Artist

This catalogue has been published to accompany the exhibition
Richard Deacon *Out of Order*   14 May – 25 September 2005
Essays by Clarrie Wallis and Edmund de Waal
ISBN 1 85437 584 9
A catalogue record for this publication is available from the British Library
© Tate Trustees 2005 all rights reserved
All works © the artist   All photography © the photographers
Edited by Susan Daniel-McElroy, Sara Hughes and Kerry Rice
Design by Andrew Smith   Repro and print by Jigsaw, Leeds
Tate St Ives Photography by Marcus Leith and Andrew Dunkley © Tate
This project has been supported by the Henry Moore Foundation
With additional support from Tate St Ives' Members

Front and back cover
Details from **Restless**
2005
Steamed ash and stainless steel
158 x 374 x 257 cm
Courtesy Lisson Gallery, London
© the Artist

Inside back flap
Detail from **Infinity #28**
2005
Stainless steel
190 x 160 x 5 cm
Courtesy Lisson Gallery, London
© the Artist